Notes to a Violinist

A Developmental Guide for Violinists & Teachers

Jan Mark Sloman

Notes to a Violinist

by Jan Mark Sloman

Book cover and interior design by Smashed-Grid Studio

Front cover photograph by Jacob Sloman

Back cover photograph by Tarisio

Published in Dallas, Texas

ISBN: 979-8-9947850-0-3 (print)

979-8-9947850-1-0 (epub)

Library of Congress Control Number: 2026903085

Table of Contents

A Personal Note with Acknowledgments

My husband, Jan Mark Sloman, passed away September 27, 2022. He had just finished writing and doing preliminary editing of this book, which he had thought about writing for multiple decades.

Numerous teachers had asked him to write a book to explain how he had produced so many students who played at such a high level. Students had also suggested that he write a book that they could use as a reference as they pursued their professional or amateur careers.

Over the years, Jan had written notes as he thought about art, music, the violin, teaching, and life itself. He pinned the notes to the bulletin board above his desk in his violin studio. In 2020, as the pandemic began, Jan collected these notes and began to devote his spare time to writing this book.

I would like to thank people who played key roles in the process of seeing this book to publication. I will do my best to acknowledge those who supported Jan while he was alive and those who supported me in my best effort to see that his book was published after his death.

Thank you to Jaime Laredo for writing the beautiful Introduction. It captures their unique relationship that evolved over six decades from student/teacher to friend to colleague.

Thank you to Yo-Yo Ma, Itzhak Perlman, and Ida Kavafian for writing wonderful endorsements of the book. All three were Jan's friends from his teenage years and became professional colleagues. He loved sharing thoughts about music and teaching with them as each pursued rewarding lives in music.

Thank you to former students Susan Gillis and Eun-song Koh for helping organize and edit the book. Susan was instrumental in the early stages of editing while Jan was alive. Eun-song sat with Jan on weekends as he played with his thoughts, discussed them, and organized them on the page.

Thank you to Matilde Stolfa, an excellent professional photographer, for taking the photos of Shannon Lee that illustrate important points that Jan chose Shannon to model. Thank you to Kevin Lee for his graphics.

Thank you to Jacob Sloman for taking the photograph for the book cover, which showed Jan in his violin studio in front of the notes on the bulletin board from which the book sprang. Jacob also suggested the title for the book, *Notes to a Violinist*, well-aware of his father's fondness for puns as well as for music.

Thank you to Bruce Sloman for offering advice and encouragement as the project began. Thanks to others who made contributions during editing but preferred to remain anonymous.

The most important organizing and editing contributions were made by the tireless efforts of two of Jan's former students and teaching assistants, sisters Shannon Lee and Jordan Lee. Both studied with Jan for many years. They made sure that this book would be the best reflection of Jan Sloman and his commitment to the art of teaching the violin and self-expression through music. Without their selflessness and determination, this book might not have been self-published. I can never thank them enough.

Louise Sloman

Introduction

The first time I ever met Jan Sloman was at the Meadowmount School of Music in the summer of 1960. Jan was this incredibly adorable 11-year-old who had started to study with Sally Thomas at the Juilliard Prep, and I was just finishing my studies with Ivan Galamian and starting a career. I can still see and hear Jan as a young boy playing the Allegro by Fiocco at a concert in front of all of his colleagues. He had such joy in his playing and seemed to be having the time of his life! I was also struck by the big sound that this little kid produced and his beautiful position. Everything seemed so natural and organic!

About 10 years went by before I met Jan again. I started teaching at the Curtis Institute of Music in 1971, and lo and behold, Jan was in my first class of students there. I shared all the students with Mr. Galamian, the idea being that they had a lesson with him one week and a lesson with me the next. I loved it, of course, because I had the opportunity to work with all these great Galamian students. I loved teaching Jan because he was always so enthusiastic and so eager to learn!

After Jan left Curtis, I again did not see him for a number of years. We resumed our relationship when he got the position of associate concertmaster of the Dallas Symphony. I played with the symphony very often and of course spent a great deal of time with Jan. It was so nice because our relationship had changed so much; we were no longer teacher and student, but rather friends and colleagues. I remember so many memorable times of great meals, scotch, and fine wines. Both Jan and I really enjoyed the good life!

It was during the Dallas days that I realized how devoted Jan was to his teaching. We spent *so* much time talking about his students, and on more than one occasion, he had them play for me or would give me a tape of someone's playing that he was particularly fond of.

When I started to teach at the Cleveland Institute of Music in 2012, I asked Jan if he had any students that might be interested in coming to Cleveland to work with me. That following February, when we held our auditions, Jan sent four or five students. As things turned out, they were without a doubt some of the best players that we heard. I remember during a lunch break, Joel Smirnoff, who was then President of the school and a member of the violin faculty, came up to me very excitedly and asked me, "Who is this guy Jan Sloman? His kids are incredible." I told him about Jan, and he said, "Do you think we could get him here?" I spoke to Jan and asked him if he had any interest in coming to Cleveland. He didn't think that he would want to leave Dallas, but maybe he might commute. Well, I put him in touch with Smirnoff, and they agreed that he would fly to Cleveland every two weeks and spend a few days teaching. Thereafter, we shared many students, just like I had done with Galamian many years before at Curtis.

I absolutely loved working with Jan. He was so devoted to the students and cared so much for them in every way. We spent hours talking about them, what they were working on, and all the problems they faced. Our wonderful meals that we had together in Dallas continued in Cleveland!

Jan taught at the Cleveland Institute for only a few years but he left a great legacy. He is missed by everyone, but no one misses him more than I do. I treasure the years that we spent teaching together as a team.

Jaime Laredo
September 2023

Editorial Note

By the fall of 2022, Jan Sloman had all but finished the manuscript for this book (then titled *The Sloman Method*). It began with the Foreword and ended with Closing Notes, including rough placeholders for images throughout. We have tried to remain as faithful as possible to his original text, editing for clarity only where necessary. We added photo captions, footnotes, the "About the Author" section (adapted from his website), and the appendix of additional commentary at the end; and labeled the sections of repertoire lists in Part III for organizational clarity. The musical and rhythmical examples that Sloman had provided through photographs have been rendered in musical notation, as well as a few measures of reference for the beginning of each etude mentioned in the "Abbreviated Condensed Etude Sequence" (ACES) section. It should be noted that the numbering of etudes referenced in ACES coincides with the editions from International Music Company (IMC) – particularly Ivan Galamian's editions of the five books: *42 Studies* by Rodolphe Kreutzer; *36 Etudes or Caprices* by Federigo Fiorillo; *24 Caprices* by Jacques Pierre Rode; *24 Studies* by Pierre Gaviniès; and *24 Etudes and Caprices,* Opus 35 by Jakob Dont. The fingerings and bowings in these sample measures are not representative of those found in the IMC editions, but rather come from a variety of public domain editions. In the scale acceleration and vibrato acceleration exercises, and in certain ACES etudes, we also added a few musically notated examples to help explain Sloman's descriptions. Regarding the Sloman Scale Chart, it may be helpful to mention that the book *Scale System – Scale Exercises in All Major and Minor Keys for Daily Study* by Carl Flesch was a resource often recommended by Sloman as a starting point for finding scales, arpeggios, and double stops written out in each key.

Shannon Lee

Notes to a Violinist

Foreword

Over more than six decades I have had a long and multifaceted career with the violin. Early on, I experienced different schools of structural training, from Franco Belgian to Dounis, as well as others in between. I attended Juilliard Prep, was a University Scholar at Princeton University, and attended the Curtis Institute of Music. I have been a concertmaster in Florence, Pittsburgh, Geneva, Lugano, Melbourne, and Dallas. I have worked with Carlos Kleiber, Lorin Maazel, and Yehudi Menuhin, as well as Tony Bennett, Ray Charles, John Williams, and Henry Mancini. I have played major violin concertos with orchestra and chamber music with Leonard Rose; recorded film soundtracks; worked with Willie Nelson; and played and drummed until dawn at Latin Fest.

I was fortunate to receive this rigorous and useful information, but in looking back, realize how much more could have been achieved by the teacher fully accepting their responsibility to create the kind of positive relationship with the student that can allow and nurture both their maximum violinistic as well as personal benefit. The kind of teaching that instead creates significant obstacles to be overcome—humiliation, condescension, and anxiety—represents the teacher's irresponsible lack of understanding, and can no longer be tolerated.

The following is a systematic method that I have thought about and used for over thirty years. It has been demonstrably effective. Though it is rigorous and thorough, it is not meant to be inflexible.

Much of the work that needs to be done to be prepared for this highly competitive violin world is the tough, lonely, hours-in-the-practice-room process I call ABT: Acquisition of Big Technique. This rigorous and thorough process, largely devoted to scales, etudes, and technical studies is the basis for anything a performer will do on the violin. Great technical ability is the underpinning for both artistic and professional success. "Art is work and not inspiration; invention comes with craft."—Stephen Sondheim. To this is added appropriate repertoire—always including unaccompanied Bach—that is given in a sequence dictated by both the developmental needs and current abilities of a particular student's circumstances.

Knowing when to assign repertoire that is appropriate is one of teaching's biggest challenges. This changes with each student. It is very much like constructing a building: first comes the combined vision of both architect and client, followed by plans, and finished with construction under correct guidelines. Many teachers seem content to choose wallpaper and light fixtures before pouring the concrete foundation. Students must be given both proper technical and artistic training, and teachers must be willing to direct this hard, demanding, unglamorous work to bring it all together.

This is a critical time in the history of the violin. Teachers must resist the temptation to exploit the general demand for sizzle and above all make sure that the steak is well prepared. Teaching systems must be adjusted to serve each individual student, or, as Amos Bronson Alcott once said, "The true teacher defends his pupils against his own personal influence."

The kind of teaching that resembles cloning—"Don't think! Play like me, teach like me!"—is no longer viable. Only informed teaching can help create the prepared and independent violinists who will successfully meet the challenges of music in the 21st century.

The learning process involves developing skills that enable both competence and creativity. The acquisition and continuing development of both "enthusiasm and order" (Paul Valéry) creates the greatest possibility for any performer's most powerful artistry.

Robust technical achievement must always be placed in the context of its goal: each player's maximum ability for musical expression. Ignoring this aspect of our art is both naive and unrealistic.

The body learns by repetition. Practice is best when that repetition is both productive and directed. All technical exercises are part of developing performing excellence. Focusing on these elements during practice is essential.

While understanding the spiritual and cerebral elements of music making, one must also acknowledge the "athletic" aspect of playing. Repetition by itself is not enough. Mindful repetition must be done correctly and over a long enough period for the body to understand what is being asked of it. Athletes at all levels of achievement understand this. Practicing slowly, correctly, and with adequate repetition allows the body to learn in its own way. This most productive kind of work is best thought of as Performance Preparation Exercise (PPE).

Good performance always contains discernible complexity involving the whole being, both physical and artistic. Achieving excellence requires the performer to understand and manifest this necessity. It is the teacher's responsibility to inculcate the understanding of these values. By establishing and insisting on healthy developmental parameters while rejecting rigidity and orthodoxy, the teacher helps the student create their own gradus ad Parnassum (steps towards mastery). What each performer hears and communicates will be different. This purity of true artistic intent is both expressive and powerful. Our current culture can lead away from this focus, making performance frenetic, visually exhausting—and joyless.

Teachers must understand this juxtaposition of the current competitive culture with purity of artistic intent and performance. They must make sure that students understand the musical possibilities of the expressive aural traditions of our instrument that can enrich and enhance individual artistry. A healthy performing presence projects confidence and shows achievement without affectation. The goal for both teacher and student is always creation.

Motivation

A degree of motivation is necessary for progress and eventual success. It is the teacher's responsibility to nurture and encourage it in each student. Abusive teaching may once have been the norm, but no more. Teachers hold great responsibility for both excellence and failure. Taking that responsibility seriously must be part of every teacher's commitment to both students and self.

Instinct

It is intellectual understanding through adequate and informed repetition, using both aural and muscular pathways, that makes possible the creation of instinct. Preparation is best understood as the means to the goal of successful performance.

A healthy and rigorous etude series—structured, executed, and well-achieved—is the key to performing excellence. The logical progression described here is meant to build one level of achievement upon another with increasingly challenging difficulty. The effort is rewarded by improvement in the execution of appropriate repertoire choices.

Anxiety

Focused preparation, including scales and etudes, is the key to releasing the grip of anxiety. Mindless hours-long repetition is not a solution. All practice is Performance Preparation Exercise (PPE). Repetitive Correct Motion (RCM) is the true PPE. This method can also be thought of as "playing fast slowly."

Remember: Intellect informs instinct. Great PPE starts as intellectual understanding and, through focused RCM, becomes instinct.

A good and effective teacher must make these necessary steps clear and must also possess the ability to have the patience and perspicacity to guide the student through the process over time. This is a great responsibility that needs to be taken seriously. Each student needs their own goal-oriented process. The progression in this book offers guidance and parameters that include both specificity and flexibility.

I have notes on this book stretching back nearly thirty years. After having heard from colleagues and former students expressing their interest in the project, I am convinced that it will be a useful developmental guide for both teachers and performers. I view successful violin teaching as results based and can say with confidence that this method not only works, but that it also can be used for all students regardless of their age or goals.

Key Terms

RCM Repetitive Correct Motion

AR Adequate Repetition

PPE Performance Preparation Exercises

ACES Abbreviated Condensed Etude Sequence

PARRQ Pitch, Articulation, Rhythm, Relationship, Quality

ABT Acquisition of Big Technique

FFAS Fourth Finger Avoidance Syndrome

Resident Resonance refers to each violin's acoustic capacity

Notes on Practice

Slow, broad, meticulous practice that *always* uses RCM (Repetitive Correct Motion) allows the student to develop the understanding needed for technical excellence through consistent engagement of correct ear/hand/muscle procedures. Practice always needs to be driven mentally while being expressed physically. The increased understanding of the physical processes needed for correct sound parameters—bow speed, position, point of contact, hair exposure, using good ergonomics—helps the student gain more of the violin's acoustic capacity, making possible its best Resident Resonance.

This work, done with patience and persistence, leads to performing excellence.

Each note should contain PARRQ:

- Pitch
- Articulation
- Rhythm
- Relationship
- Quality

Situating these elements (PARRQ) in the context of a lyric continuum allows the musical line to contain inflection, nuance, and flow. The student needs to grow to accept, respect, and enjoy this process. Embracing productive repetition teaches the player the value of a healthy routine that limits disruption.

Excellent performance can be achieved when the player is able to understand the music's over-arching rhythmic and technical framework, making possible true artistic poise and control. This gives the student the freedom to not only conceive what they want to hear but also to create it.

Using correct ergonomics and alignment—ensuring that the larger muscle groups support the smaller ones—allows for preparation/practice to emphasize relaxation. Working positively with parameters that have been internalized by RCM and excellent ergonomics give the performer the ability to consider the violin as a vehicle for great performance rather than an obstacle. Possessing these abilities gives huge capability for expression. It is not a quaint anachronism—with focused work, music can be made through the violin regardless of its challenges. It is important to understand that healthy habits must be formed, and that challenges can be overcome if good solutions are understood and implemented. The process used in development of overall technique must always be designed and directed towards achieving the technical excellence that enables real musical achievement.

The stages of preparation include:

1. Okay

2. Good

3. Great

4. Excellent

Categories of practice/preparation:

1. Formative learning using correct initial practice procedures

2. Slow, hard-wiring practice via RCM

3. Performance (requires repetition with focus on the goal; adequate time spent on #2 facilitates #3)

Listening and analyzing recorded performances gives the student and teacher an important resource to further increase dynamic and expressive range.

Part I:

Scales, Arpeggios, and Double Stops

Scales

The following sequence of scales, right- and left-hand exercises, and double stops is a good foundation for all technical achievement. This system is not meant to be inflexible. When done with repetitive *correct* motion (RCM) it gives a wide range of choices for both teacher and student.

In my experience the consistent and excellent practice of scales and etudes provides the best possible kind of injury prevention. By using RCM the surrounding muscles, ligaments, and tendons are strengthened and aligned in both the left and right hand. While accepting the notion of appropriate muscular involvement, ergonomic balance gives the player the ability to inculcate maximum relaxation while minimizing unnecessary tension.

Begin with the scale using the whole bow, 4 beats @ 60 BPM.[1] It is important to keep in mind the right-hand finger position and left-hand alacrity (finger lifting and dropping), while always remembering to vibrate! Use the entire muscle chain of the right arm to continuously maintain the character and quality of sound even as more notes are added to each beat.

---

[1] Beats per minute

Scale Acceleration Exercise

Scale Acceleration Exercise in A Major

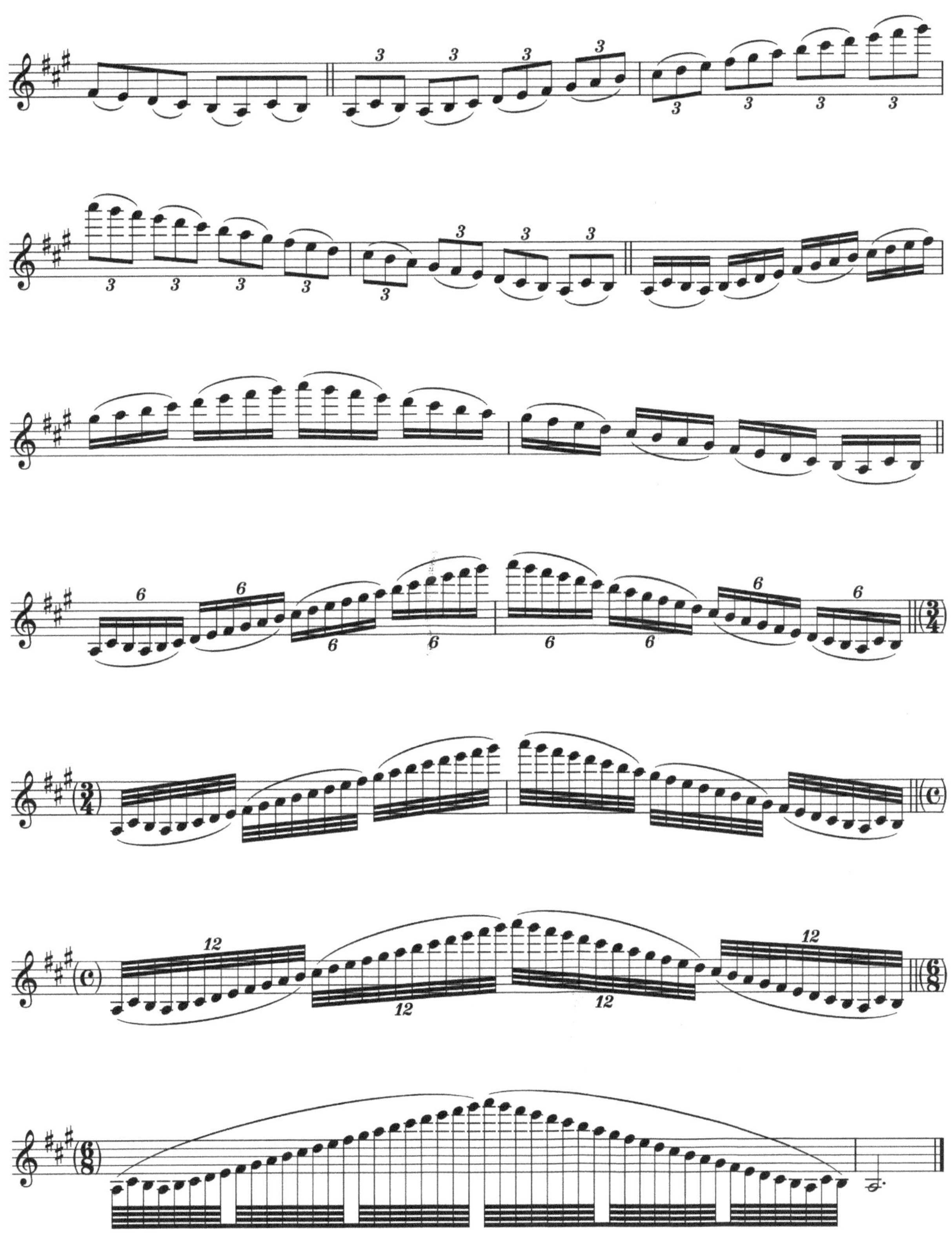

Posture ....

Make sure that the larger muscles are ergonomically placed to support the smaller muscle groups. This distribution of energy makes possible maximum relaxation and freedom of the mechanisms used to play the violin—shoulder, arm, wrist, and fingers.

Holding the violin up is crucial but is best achieved in the larger context of holding the torso in a good position that receives the violin.

Notes to a Violinist

General posture holding the violin

Practice 3-octave scales. A 4th octave can be added to scales up to C.

Example in 4 octaves: A Major Scale

Left Hand ....

It is very important to use vibrato during all scale practice.

Continuous vibrato needs to be developed as the default mechanism. Using the correct hand position allows the performer to choose not to vibrate. Practicing with continuous vibrato allows the performer to achieve a good left-hand position that makes vibrato an artistic choice. Practicing without vibrato puts the left hand in a different position that requires change in order to vibrate. Developing the vibrato which only functions with delay breaks up the musical line and puts a "belly" in the middle of each stroke. The "wah wah" sound created with this kind of vibrato is part of the sound one hears attending a "NASCAR" racing event. Its use in violin playing and music making is at best questionable.

Rotation of the joint (closest to the fingertip) that occurs in vibrato

Striking the string with crisp and consistent motion using the pad of the finger is important for both clarity and intonation (see Kreutzer No. 9 on page 47). It is very important that the same crisp vertical motion be used to lift the finger as well. Remember that the fingers have more landing room on the lower side of the string. This better activates the finger pad and helps to create correct left-hand position.

Notes to a Violinist

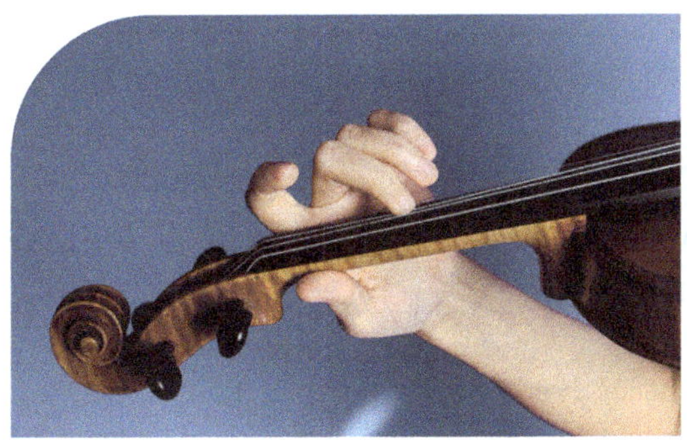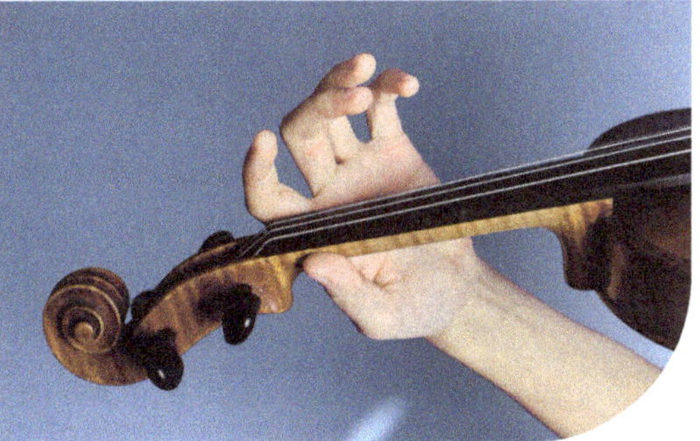

Illustration of the hand before and after finger lifting

Use all four fingers of the left hand when practicing scales—the fourth finger is no exception. Not using the fourth finger means losing 25% of the left hand's capacity. (This is akin to an eight-cylinder car using only six cylinders.) Using the fourth finger from the start of an intelligent developmental process makes sense in every way: strength, flexibility, expressive capabilities, alacrity, hand position—and survival.

Shifting should be calculated, calm, and consistent. Whether a shift is primarily made for transportation or expression is determined by its lyric context. Shifting always contains three parts: 1) note of departure → 2) the journey → 3) note of arrival.

There are three basic choices: old-bow shift, new-bow shift, and between-bow shift.

- ❧ Old-bow shift: accomplished on the note of departure
- ❧ New-bow shift: on the note of arrival
- ❧ Between-bow shift: during the bow change (silent)

It is important to feel the destination position before commencing the shift.

Vibrato ....

Think from the left hand and play with the right, as if vibrato activates the bow. Always remember that vibrato travels from the pitch, below the pitch, and back to the pitch. It should *never* go over the pitch, since the ear hears that as playing sharp.

Practice any continuous sixteenth work (Kreutzer No. 2, for example) in octaves, 4 beats at 60 BPM.

The left-hand position should be relaxed, enabling the fingers of the left hand to move down and up with alacrity. This develops correctly with the use of adequate RCM.

Excerpt from the beginning of Kreutzer's Etude No. 2:

Expanded in octaves:

Vibrato Acceleration Exercise

This exercise can be applied to scale practice.

I.e., in an A Major scale:

Vibrate at increasing rates of alternation between the pitch itself and slightly below the pitch.

etc. (every other note above is slightly lower than the actual pitch)

Right Hand ....

Bow direction is best when it is perpendicular to the string.

Pulling and pushing the bow (down-bow about 10:30 and up-bow 1:30, as on the diagram below) creates the horizontal energy needed to best activate the violin's resident resonance, enabling more seamless bow changes.

Bow distribution works best with good right-arm position. Think of seven possible planes in space across which the bow moves.

1. E string

2. A string

3. D string

4. G string

5. G & D

6. D & A

7. A & E

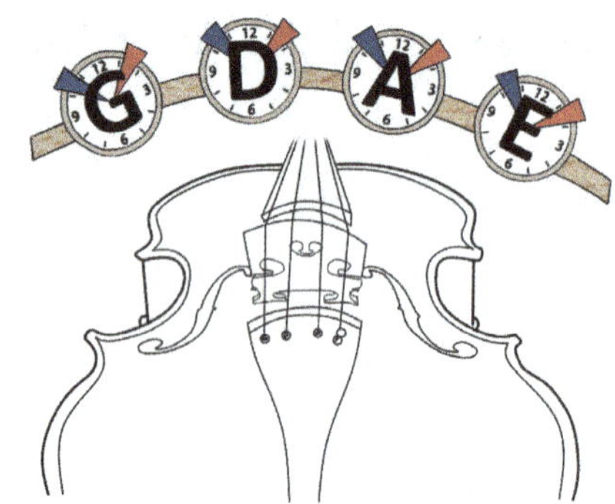

Each row from top, left to right: position of bow at E string only, A string only;
D string only; G string only

*Each row from top, left to right: position of bow at G&D strings,
D&A strings, A&E strings*

The angle of the bow hair, flattish in general, can be adjusted depending on the timbre desired.

It is important to know that the fingers in the right hand, though extremely participatory, are not necessarily proactive. Think of using the right-hand finger pads to engage the string, which will allow the vibrations created to be felt by the performer.

Control of bow speed during bow changes allows for seamless linear phrasing. String crossings can best be executed towards a goal position on the subsequent string. It is also possible to prepare the right-arm position for that next note.

Rhythms ....

Rhythms can be useful when done correctly, particularly noting the crisp strike and abrupt lift of the fingers of the left hand.[2]

---

[2] Rhythms are most useful when practiced with their "opposites," in balanced groups of related patterns.

Martelé ....

Martelé requires the use of an arm position largely unsupported by the body's physiology. This motion, correctly executed, is a very important part of right-arm control. A difficult and complicated stroke, it is best described as being like the word "bop." (It starts with controlled capture of the string, followed by release and motion with speed and energy, ending with the starting point for the next stroke.) The elbow and arm position must be consistent for each string, enabling the open and close motion of the forearm. The down bow should largely be executed using the triceps, and the up bow with the biceps.

Play the scale using upper half and lower half martelé.[3]

Essential Mixed Bowings (start down or up bow)

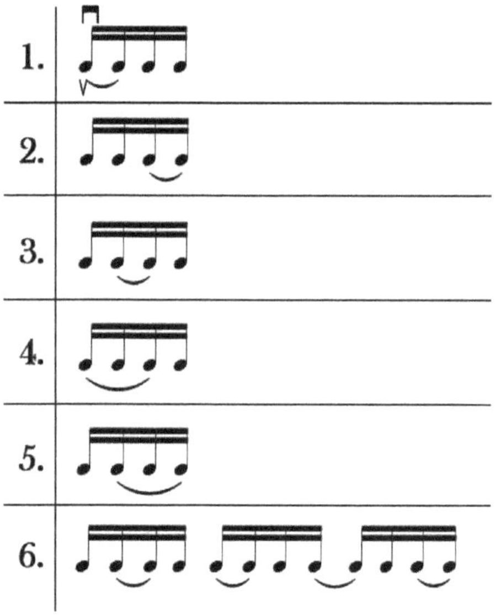

1.
2.
3.
4.
5.
6.

---

[3] Martelé in the upper half (UH) or lower half (LH) of the bow

Images of a down-bow double martelé stroke, starting from the frog,
stopping in the middle; then starting from the middle and stopping at the tip

Bow Sweeps ....

A bow sweep can be thought of as a martelé stroke with "BO" and no "P" ("BO" not "BOP").

Practice/play on open strings, doing several repetitions on each string. Play a few up bows, a few down bows, and a few alternating up bow and down bow.

Play the scale with "bow sweeps."

Suggested sequence for scale practice

1. Martelé, UH & LH[4]

2. Frog motion (to be done at the extreme frog with correct and supportive arm position) in two-note slurs

3. Martelé bowings with slurs #1–6 (see previous page)

4. Bow sweeps

Systematically apply bowings over rhythms, as needed, to remedy specific problems of repertoire through complication.

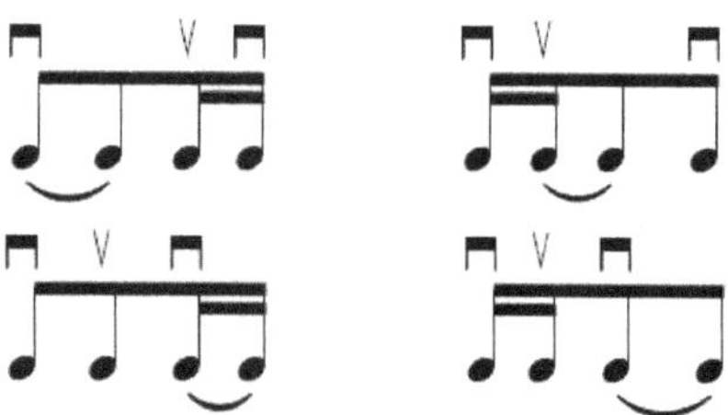

---

[4] Upper half (UH) or lower half (LH) of the bow

Sloman Scale Chart ....

The table below is printed in landscape (rotated) orientation. Day numbers 1–28 are the columns; each practice type is a row. Uppercase = major keys, lowercase = minor keys. Split into two parts by day range.

Days 1–14

	1	2	3	4	5	6	7	8	9	10	11	12	13	14
Scales	C	E	eb	F	c#	Gb	Db	g	d	Ab	f#	Eb	f#	c
Arpeggios	Eb	B	G	A	Gb	F	A	Db	F#	C	F#	D	Bb	Gb
1 8va Scales/Arpeggios	b	g	Gb	d	F	C#	E	bb	G	Eb	ab	c#	e	D
Octaves	F#	bb	C	eb	D	e	f#	a	b	c#	F	G	d	g
2nds	A	f#	B	c#	Ab	Bb	C#	F#	F#	f	D	b	Gb	a
4ths	G	C	ab	Bb	Eb	d	B	c	D	e	c#	F#	Ab	bb
3rds	D	c#	Eb	C#	a	A	c	Gb	a	Bb	C	ab	c#	f
6ths	B	Gb	A	D	F#	E	g	c#	Db	c	b	Db	Eb	C#
Fingered Octaves	c#	a	f	ab	b	f#	D	Eb	e	F#	c	bb	g	eb
10ths	E	c#	f	e	c#	b	ab	B	[illegible]	[illegible]	[illegible]	[illegible]	[illegible]	[illegible]
(unlabeled)	Db	a	Bb	c	E	eb	F	f	[illegible]	[illegible]	[illegible]	[illegible]	[illegible]	[illegible]
(unlabeled)	Gb	eb	f#	b	C	c#	f#	D	[illegible]	[illegible]	[illegible]	[illegible]	[illegible]	[illegible]
(unlabeled)	f	Ab	c#	G	bb	C	eb	ab	[illegible]	[illegible]	[illegible]	[illegible]	[illegible]	[illegible]
(unlabeled)	ab	D	c#	f#	G	g	Bb	C#	[illegible]	[illegible]	[illegible]	[illegible]	[illegible]	[illegible]

Days 15–28

	15	16	17	18	19	20	21	22	23	24	25	26	27	28
Scales	F#	f	D	e	C#	G	c#	A	bb	B	ab	b	Bb	a
Arpeggios	E	C#	B	D	Ab	E	C	Eb	C#	Db	G	Bb	F	Ab
1 8va Scales/Arpeggios	c	f#	F#	Db	A	c#	Ab	Bb	B	f	C	f#	a	eb
Octaves	f	A	ab	c	f#	Eb	Bb	Db	Gb	C#	B	Ab	c#	E
2nds	eb	E	G	C	c	bb	f#	c#	ab	Eb	Db	e	g	d
4ths	f#	Gb	C#	a	b	f#	eb	g	f	D	e	c#	E	F
3rds	B	d	f#	b	G	F#	g	E	eb	F	bb	Db	f#	Bb
6ths	Ab	bb	e	F	eb	ab	f	d	C	G	f#	a	c#	f#
Fingered Octaves	G	Ab	f	Gb	Db	B	E	F	e	a	Bb	C	A	C#
10ths	[illegible]	[illegible]	[illegible]	[illegible]	[illegible]	[illegible]	[illegible]	[illegible]	[illegible]	[illegible]	[illegible]	[illegible]	[illegible]	Db
(unlabeled)	[illegible]	[illegible]	[illegible]	[illegible]	[illegible]	[illegible]	[illegible]	[illegible]	[illegible]	[illegible]	[illegible]	[illegible]	[illegible]	f#
(unlabeled)	[illegible]	[illegible]	[illegible]	[illegible]	[illegible]	[illegible]	[illegible]	[illegible]	[illegible]	[illegible]	[illegible]	[illegible]	[illegible]	G
(unlabeled)	[illegible]	[illegible]	[illegible]	[illegible]	[illegible]	[illegible]	[illegible]	[illegible]	[illegible]	[illegible]	[illegible]	[illegible]	[illegible]	Eb
(unlabeled)	[illegible]	[illegible]	[illegible]	[illegible]	[illegible]	[illegible]	[illegible]	[illegible]	[illegible]	[illegible]	[illegible]	[illegible]	[illegible]	B

The horizontal numbers represent a 28-day sequence. Each day, considered vertically, includes different keys for scale practice (uppercase: major keys, lowercase: minor keys). This method of practice adds a useful and important level of concentration to the overall concept of scale practice.

Arpeggios

Continuous and regular work on arpeggios is of great importance. It has impact on intonation, shifting, vibrato, left-hand position, and developing a crisp lift and drop motion with the left-hand fingers. Practicing arpeggios creates a logical and predictable frame within which the left hand can operate.

Example: A Major Arpeggio

Practice each arpeggio with rhythms 1–4 listed below.

Examples 1–4 are an acceleration exercise to be executed using continuous vibrato. Number 1 and number 2 can be played with separate bows, number 3 is played with three notes to a bow, and number 4 is three octaves in one bow. Rhythms (e.g., and) can be useful in helping to create alacrity but must be done with consistently and crisply executed vertical motion in the left-hand fingers. When shifting, use correct hand position and always keep in mind that accuracy is the goal, not speed.

Double Stops

Working on double stops organizes and strengthens the left hand. Make sure that the left elbow position is relaxed and consistently positioned beneath the left hand in such a way that there is no strain from either the left or the right. Think of the left elbow being positioned in alignment with the left hand.

The value of advanced finger placement (double stops) is especially strong in string crossings. It is valuable not only in bringing the two strings closer together on the same plane, but also allows for improved intonation.

There is a plane for each of the four strings and three planes (GD, DA, AE) for double stops.

*The left hand in double-stop fingerings on the strings G&D (left) and D&A (right)
and corresponding elbow position*

*The left hand in various double-stop fingerings on the strings
A&E and corresponding elbow position*

Note: *It is extremely important to vibrate on all double stops.*

Double Stops in A Major

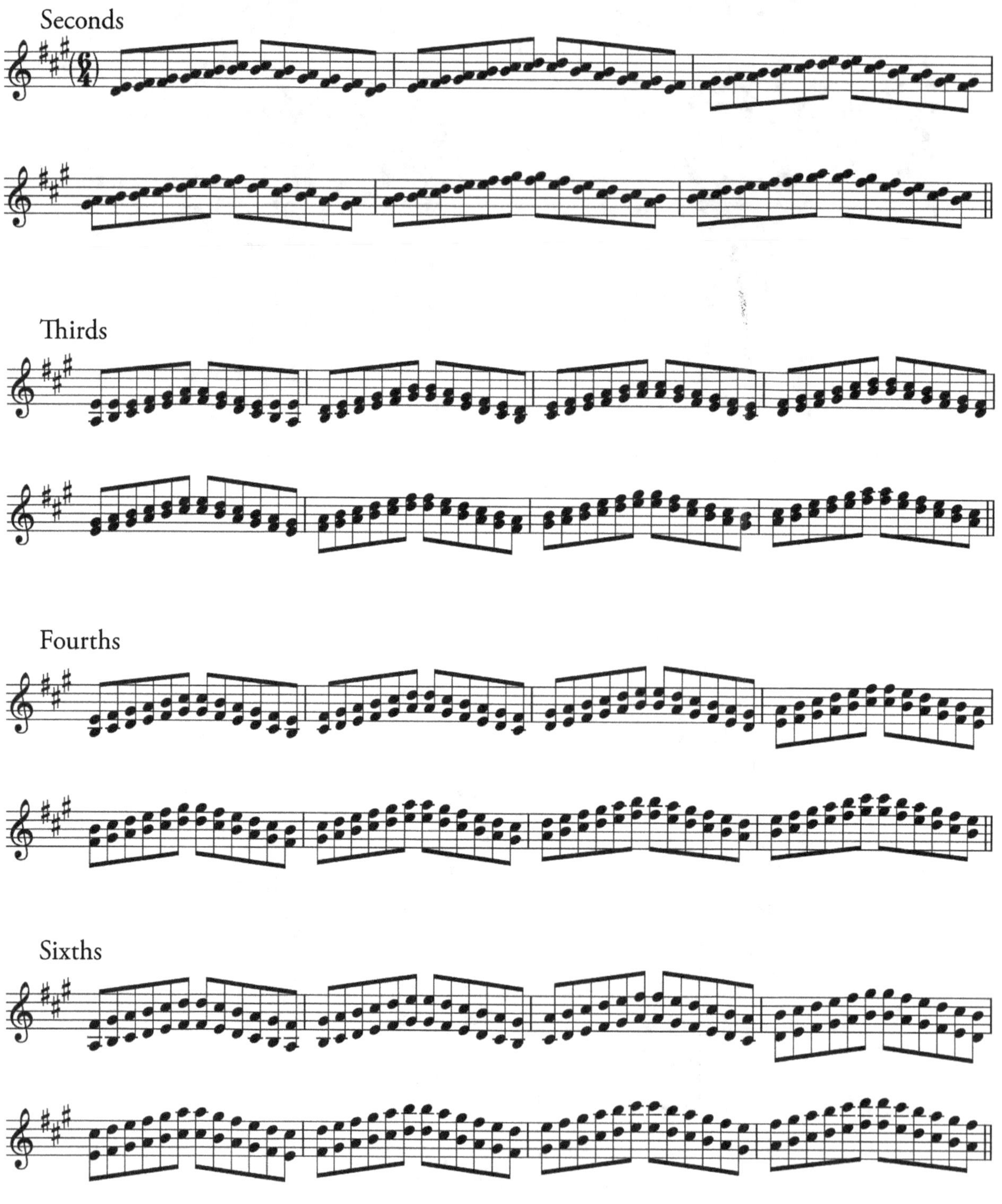

Octaves and Fingered Octaves

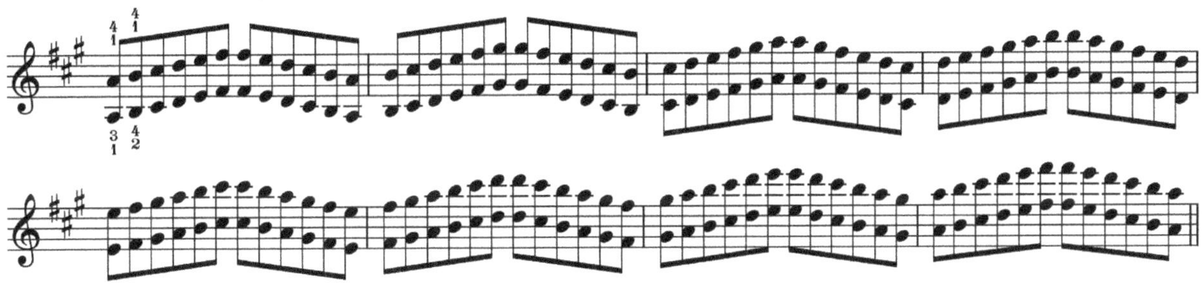

Tenths

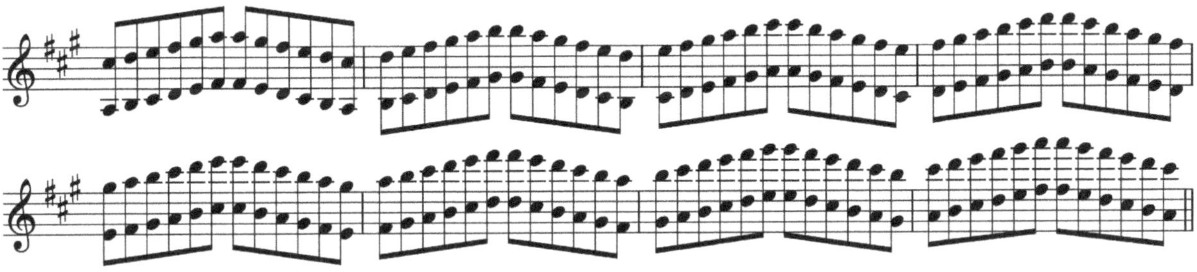

Dounis Exercises

I was introduced to Demetrius Constantine Dounis by a great teacher, colleague, and friend, Joseph Silverstein. Joey studied privately with Dounis during the time that he was a student at Curtis. He described to me his lessons with Dounis about the style and substance of Dounis's teaching, which started with listening, evaluation, and discussion, after which Dounis would write out some exercises and leave the student to work on them. The following two manuscripts and notes were given to me by Joey as examples of Dounis's teaching. They can be very useful as a part of any responsible teaching method, showing a range of structural possibilities that can be used as a starting point for creative technical exploration. Dounis taught several students at the same time in different rooms, always tailoring his process to the individual student and the challenges each presented. Lessons were frequently several hours in length. The use of Dounis exercises can be very valuable when correctly taught and executed, but Joey said that some of what he wrote was done to fulfill the contractual and financial needs of his publisher.

It is important to understand that, in general, a shift contains three parts:

- Point of departure
- Journey
- Point of arrival

Accuracy is the goal, not speed. Insist on excellence for both the note of departure and note of arrival. Make sure that the left-hand position on the string is good through the whole motion of the shift and that the left elbow maintains a relaxed and supportive position as well.

Note: *Always vibrate during Dounis exercises!* Doing so creates a hand position from which the performer can choose whether to use or forgo vibrato according to their artistic wishes, rather than technical limitations.

Notes from a lesson with Dounis

Transcription: *Balance back — don't lean forward / Don't grip head / Find balance of: left hand cradle, collar bone, side of neck / twirl fiddle 10º on each side (with rt. hand) / Fiddle not too much to left / Align left arm (hand) in angle then make fiddle fit / Keep vibrato going in all slow scale(?). / Align tailpiece end — on rib at eye — so that area rests flat on neck — whole area between chin rest posts — + not just a tiny area of rib making contact / Turn wrist left hand out more, not only in*

An example of an exercise given by Dounis in a lesson

Part II:

Etudes

Sequence of Study

The use of etudes, once an important part of violin studies, appears to have become de-emphasized in overall violin development. Lucien Capet and Konstantin Mostras, along with their student Ivan Galamian, were clear about this necessity.

Over the years, it has become clear to me that the study of etudes in a logical and sequential order is a major part of the entire process of technical development. The correct positioning of this sequence along with appropriate repertoire choices solidifies the student's ability to perform repertoire with increased technical ease, making it possible for the student to focus on artistic excellence from a position of enhanced strength and freedom.

The following order is designed to increase the student's ability not only to solve specific technical issues but also to lengthen a student's ability to concentrate over time. To accomplish good performance outcomes requires not only physical excellence but also performing stamina. This kind of endurance is an essential part not only of successful musical performance but also of any other career options a student might eventually choose that require this kind of focus.

The sequence begins at the teacher's discretion given a student's current ability, age, and work limitations. It provides a logical framework for consideration by the teacher and can include all or parts of each group of studies. **A teacher must accept the responsibility to make sure that this essential work is a major part of the student's development.**

1. **Kayser**
   Dont Op. 37 ("Little Dont")

   These are formative etudes that begin to prepare the student not only for those studies that follow but also, more importantly, to enhance and enable excellence in performance of repertoire.

2. **Kreutzer**

   Kreutzer presents the opportunity to address the need for increasing technical ability as the overall level rises.

3. Fiorillo

These etudes further develop the process that begins with Kreutzer.

4. Rode

These caprices are very important in developing the means of expression (bow speed, bow position, linear excellence).

5. Gaviniès (some repeated)

These are arguably the most important of all etudes. Extremely challenging, they develop every aspect of performance: sound, intonation, vibrato, and left-hand position. The first time through they can be played at two tempos: extremely slowly, and then a little faster. Both speeds are determined by command and cleanliness. The second time through, if the student is ready, they can be played at an even faster tempo. These etudes require great patience and focus from both student and teacher, but the effort is very much worth it.

6. Dont Op. 35 ("Big Dont")

These etudes are important in solving many of the technical challenges that will be presented by the study of the Paganini Caprices.

7. Paganini Caprices

This entire sequence is designed for a student to arrive at the study of these caprices well prepared to overcome the technical challenges they present. Using this method, the Paganini Caprices—long considered the ultimate expression of technical mastery—become a part of a continuum, not stand-alone events. This work enhances performance of all repertoire including concerto, chamber, and orchestral playing.

Abbreviated Condensed Etude Sequence

Responsible teaching must include adequate and appropriate challenges through each level of technical development. It requires focus and patience from both teacher and student. In my experience I have clearly seen the results of students having worked through this process and can say without a doubt that it works. Teaching is a results-based effort. Etude study is a substantial part of the work that must be done.

The goal for using the ACES is to build necessary solidity of the technical foundation in a collegiate/conservatory setting, representing an extraction from the etude sequence itself while also addressing the limitations of time. The sequence of these 42 etudes provides a two-semester guideline that is essential in helping the performer develop both artistic and technical endurance (concentration over time). This sequence promotes its construction and is best used after the teacher has determined the best choices to be made to maximize its impact within the consideration of a collegiate time frame.

It is challenging to determine a good starting point within this sequence. In my experience it can take a few lessons to begin to understand what student needs must be addressed. I will often start with some of the selected Kreutzer etudes that address right-hand issues as well as a few used to develop proper left-hand hygiene.

Kreutzer[5] ....

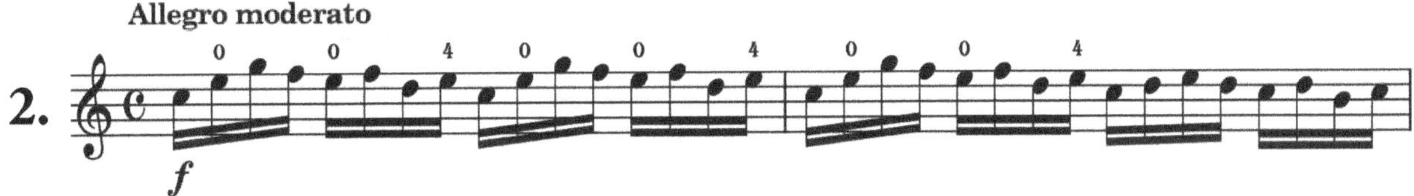

This etude is particularly good for beginning right-hand strength awareness and bow stroke development.

- **Martelé**: Can be described using the word "Bop!"— start the stroke with an attack. Move the bow quickly, perpendicular to the string. Stop the bow stroke in a position to subsequently play the next one. The release and motion are without any kind of weight or pressure from the right arm.

This etude can be useful in developing a variety of bowing styles:

- Upper half and lower half martelé (as explained above)

- **Detaché**: starting with the right arm at a 90-degree angle then opening and closing the right arm. The down-bow motion is largely controlled by the triceps, up bow with the biceps.

- Using only the fingers at the frog, play single/double/triple each note and two slurred (slowly at the extreme frog). This develops the healthy involvement of the right-hand fingers within the complete bow stroke.

---

[5] Some editions number etudes differently. See Editorial Note.

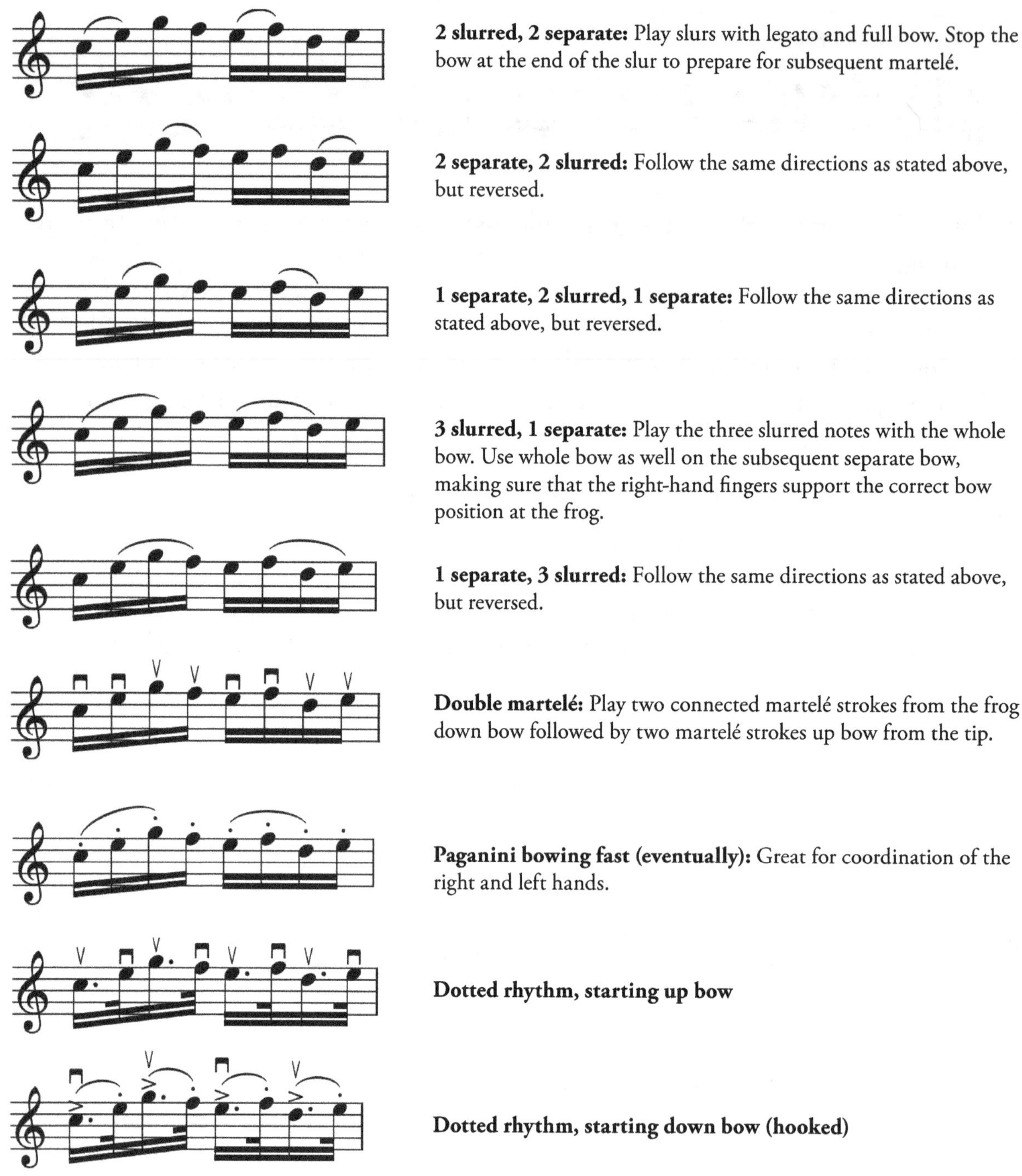

2 slurred, 2 separate: Play slurs with legato and full bow. Stop the bow at the end of the slur to prepare for subsequent martelé.

2 separate, 2 slurred: Follow the same directions as stated above, but reversed.

1 separate, 2 slurred, 1 separate: Follow the same directions as stated above, but reversed.

3 slurred, 1 separate: Play the three slurred notes with the whole bow. Use whole bow as well on the subsequent separate bow, making sure that the right-hand fingers support the correct bow position at the frog.

1 separate, 3 slurred: Follow the same directions as stated above, but reversed.

Double martelé: Play two connected martelé strokes from the frog down bow followed by two martelé strokes up bow from the tip.

Paganini bowing fast (eventually): Great for coordination of the right and left hands.

Dotted rhythm, starting up bow

Dotted rhythm, starting down bow (hooked)

Sautillé: This can be conceived as a very small and quick detaché which gains its articulation only above a certain speed. Zimbalist referred to the stroke as "laytache"; Joey Silverstein called it "medium-rare." The muscle reaction/muscle control (with adequate speed/tempo) will clarify the articulation of quicker notes.

In measures 9-11 the ascending passage (3 bars) is difficult to play in tune. Teachers should emphasize that extension fingerings are best when the motion of both fingers (finger of departure and finger of arrival) is vertical. Rolling the fingers away from their landing spot destroys the pitch.

Study number 4 should be practiced in three different ways: start up bow, start down bow, or use as a study for pizzicato.

One of the most important etudes in Kreutzer. No. 7 requires excellent bow control, bow position, bow management, and alacrity.

Play it with upper half and lower half martelé as well as collé. Make sure that the right-arm level is appropriate for the string being played and that the end of each stroke achieves the correct starting position for the subsequent bow stroke.

ॐ **Collé:** takes the smallest muscle groups and develops their useful precision and control. The basic motions involved are:

1. The vertical motion is provided by the right arm bringing the bow to a position where straightening and curling the fingers can provide the horizontal motion. The resulting sound/attack must have crystalline clarity even at the softest dynamic.

2. The horizontal motion of the stroke is provided by the right-hand fingers.

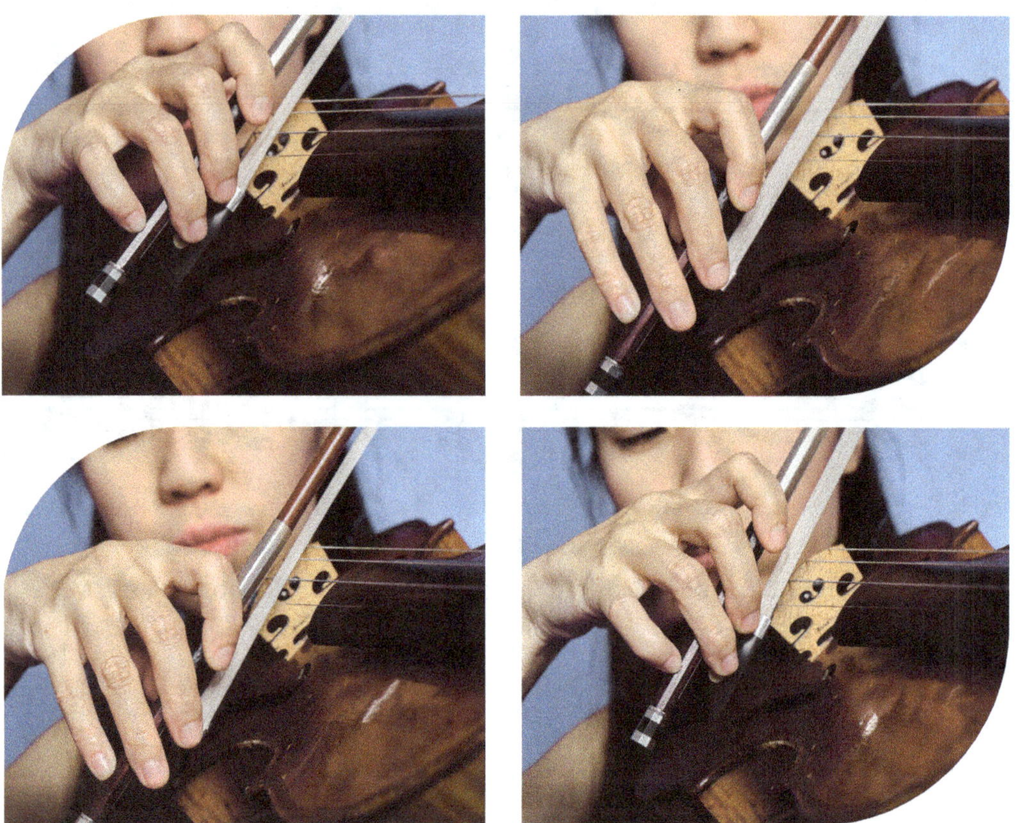

From top, left to right:

1. Collé stroke starts at the frog, from the string, with joints curled in the right hand fingers.

2. Then the fingers extend, creating the down-bow stroke, and the bow releases off slightly above the string.

3. Up-bow collé starts again from the string near the frog, this time with fingers extended.

4. Contract fingers back to the curled position to initiate the up-bow stroke, and release the bow off the string.

This etude emphasizes endurance, sound quality, and vertical left-hand finger motion. Play it slowly enough to be able to hear that everything is well in tune.

An additional exercise would be to play the etude with the fourth finger position maintained, first on the upper string (octaves) and then on the lower string (seconds).

There are two kinds of shifting: transportation and expression. Both of these shifts can be done on the old bow, the new bow, and between bows (refer to page 17 for more detailed information on shifting).

- ✌ A transportation shift is quiet, calculated, and efficient. It is not meant for expressive content.
- ✌ An expressive shift's execution and resulting sound are best determined contextually.

Make sure that all three notes of the triplet are in tune. A good left-hand position makes possible the vertical motion of the finger. Make sure that the hand position does not change. Vibrate through the entire exercise.

Think about lifting the trilling finger, not dropping. Lifting the complementary note crisply will create clarity.

Practice with rhythmically extended trills, always with good hand position.

Make sure that the grace notes are played rhythmically.

Play this etude with both regular (first and fourth fingers) and fingered (alternating first and third, second and fourth fingers) octaves. These require two different hand/finger positions that ultimately extend the left-hand position to cover the span of a fifth interval instead of the normal position (a fourth interval). Correct elbow and hand position will allow the fingers to move more vertically in fingered octaves, making possible better intonation and clearer sound. Always practice this study with vibrato.

Notes to a Violinist

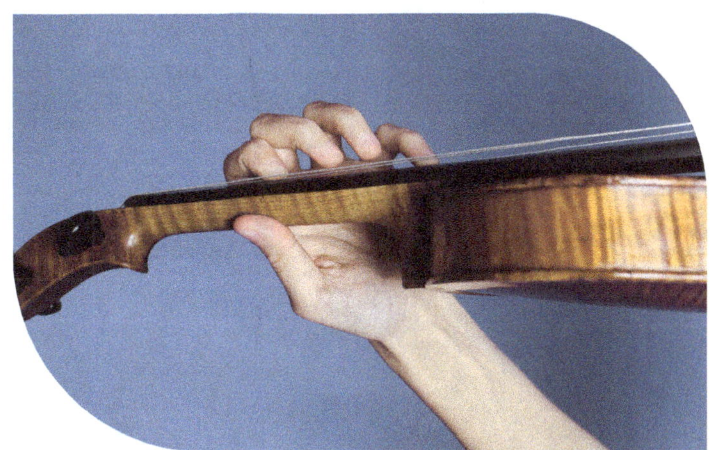

Hand and elbow position for regular octaves on D&A strings

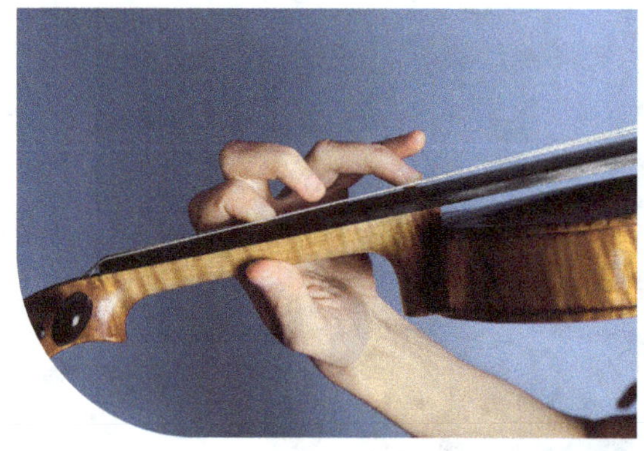
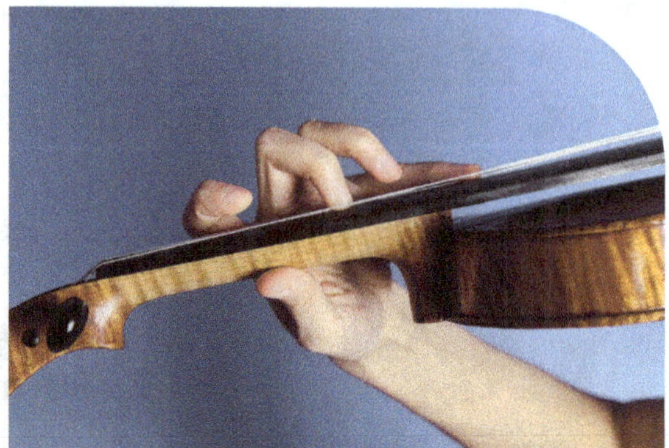

Hand and elbow position for fingered octaves on D&A strings

Play legato and always vibrate! Think of rolling the bow silently across the intervening string without lifting the bow.

Practice 1 note to a bow, then 2, then 4, then 6–8 to a bow.

Left hand: crisply lift and drop the fingers with good hand position. Work towards the goal of there being no difference in the sound and quality of articulation created by the lift or drop.

Keep the bow in contact with the string similar to what was discussed with study No. 32.

Fiorillo ....

Fiorillo etudes are transitional. They cover gaps and provide specific techniques needed before starting Rode.

This etude is similar to Kreutzer No. 4. The teacher is free to choose one or the other.

Played on all four strings, this etude is an excellent challenge for creating legato: bow speed, bow position, bow changes, variations of different vibrato characters, all with good intonation.

This study provides similar challenges as Fiorillo No. 14. It strongly emphasizes the control of the legato, especially during both the crescendo and the diminuendo.

A good way to work on this is without vibrato, using only bow speed and position to help create expressive playing that contains both nuance and dynamic control.

As the phrase tapers and the dynamic gap narrows a new phrase can emerge from the tapered space, making possible longer musical lines. It is very much like dovetailing, a woodworking technique that enables a seamless joining of two separate entities.

Dovetailing spotted in a Cleveland practice room

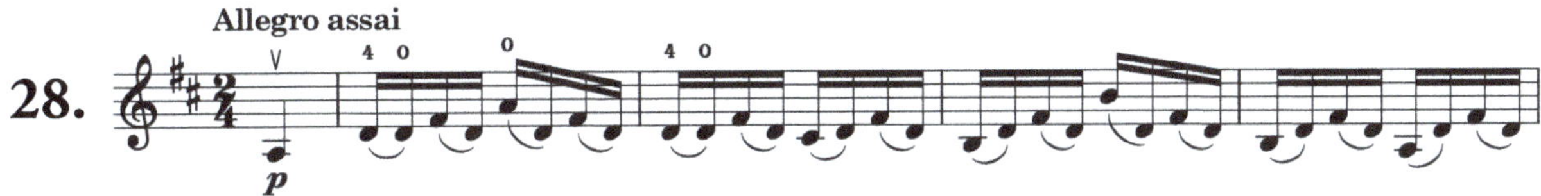

This etude should be prepared to be played very quickly and cleanly. It could be used as an audition etude or an encore work.

This is to be played with upper-half and lower-half martelé, collé, and two martelé strokes to a bow.

Rode...

These are essential studies for expression and bow control. They require understanding of bow speed, bow position, bow control, and articulation, while creating an appropriate vibrato that emphasizes the linear nature of the phrase.

No. 1 emphasizes expressive range and correct use of the bow to achieve nuance and variation within the musical line.

The second half of No. 1 is done with martelé, paying particular attention to clean attacks at the beginning of each trill.

No. 5 is virtuosic and challenges every aspect of violin playing in both the left and right hand.

Rhythmic precision, always essential, provides the framework for growth and excellence with this etude.

Notes to a Violinist

This caprice provides challenges for the player's intonation and clearly shows the level of scale preparation that has been achieved.

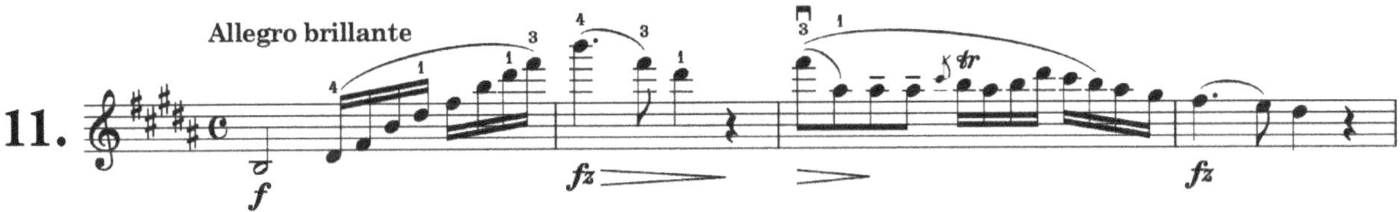

No. 11 challenges the player's intonation and requires a strong level of virtuosity to be played successfully.

This is a good study for legato and intonation, using bow speed and position, along with excellent bow changes that will make longer phrases possible.

In this ACES (Abbreviated Condensed Etude Sequence), No. 19 is a good starting point for Gaviniès. Its challenges are similar to what is coming.

Gaviniès ....

These studies might be the most important and demanding etudes for a developing violinist. They challenge virtually every aspect of technical accomplishment while enhancing the process of the emergence of a personal sound profile.

2. 

ℭℨ The focus of this etude is the discovery of the exacting and necessary precision required of both hands. Vibrated beautifully and played with excellent intonation, this study begins the process of developing the "resident resonance." Activating a sound with the strongest possibility for maximum vibration is an important component of successful performance. This etude challenges the performer's ability to maintain both focus and patience over time.

ℭℨ This study can be played at three distinct tempos:

1. Very, very slowly[6] using full bow

2. A little bit more quickly

3. A healthy Allegro

3. 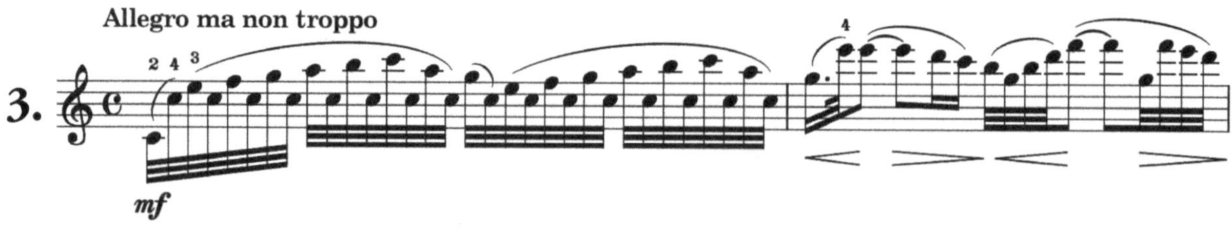

In creating good legato with the string crossings, make sure to know where on the subsequent string the bow is going, keeping the arm in a neutral position between the two strings. Use the right hand and fingers to go back and forth while maintaining a supportive position with the right arm. Make sure not to change the angle of the hair of the bow between the two strings.

---

[6] Approximately $\eighthnote = 60$

Notes to a Violinist

Given its key (D Major) this is an important study for intonation and further development of the resident resonance.

This study explores the mechanism for good intonation using extension fingerings (see Kreutzer No. 3).

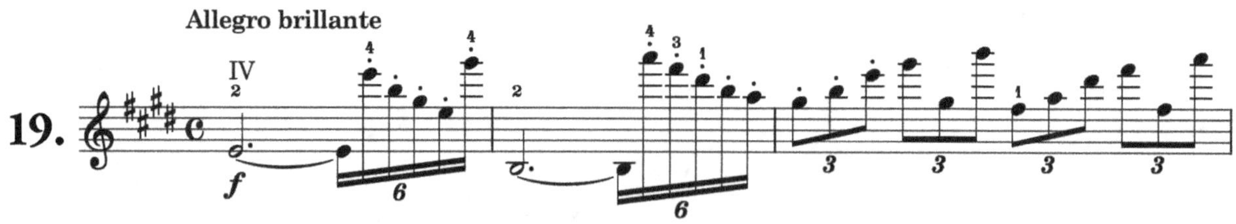

The increasing difficulty of these studies pushes the process towards its next steps.

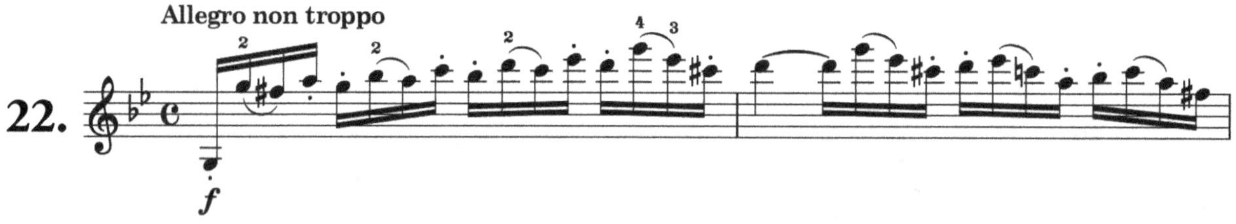

With these challenging string crossings it is important to adjust the elbow when considering the subsequent target string.

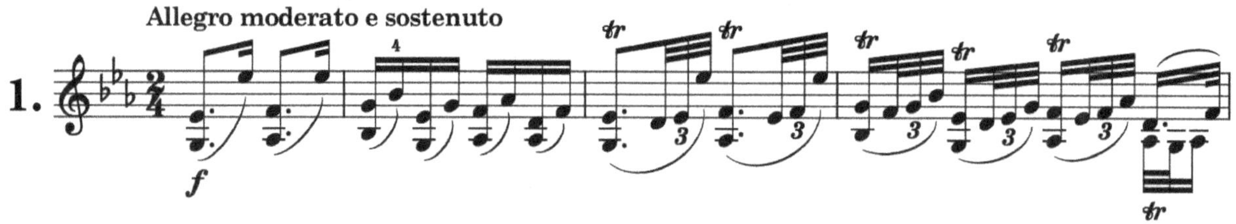

This study provides not only a recap of Gaviniès but also serves as an excellent bridge towards the challenges to come.

Notes to a Violinist

Dont Op. 35 ....

Dont Op. 35 is the developmental bridge that continues the challenges presented by Gaviniès while adding more virtuosic elements. These caprices provide an excellent final foundation for overall technical ability. They prepare the player for successfully dealing with Paganini Caprices as a part of a continuum, not a one off.

This caprice is extremely important in developing a healthy default method for playing chords.

- The three-note chord is initiated with the bow in motion. Contact with the string is made parabolically, not at a ninety-degree angle.

- The three-note chord is a flat stroke, done without dropping the elbow and with the bow following an elliptical path.

- Play this caprice both down bow and up bow. Make sure to vibrate all chords.

- With the extension fingerings at the end of the caprice the middle finger is placed in advance of the upper and lower fingers, allowing for the extension of the other fingers to be achieved more easily.

This caprice requires good left hand finger motion and position so that the strike and lift of the finger can achieve clarity.

This caprice can help develop reliable string crossings while providing exercises that emphasize the incorporation of the correct use of the hand and fingers:

- Detaché in the middle of the bow, incorporating ergonomically coordinated use of the arm, wrist, and fingers.

- Slowly at the extreme frog, with special awareness of the involvement of the fingers and the wrist.

- Tape a nickel to the tip of the bow, then play at the extreme frog.

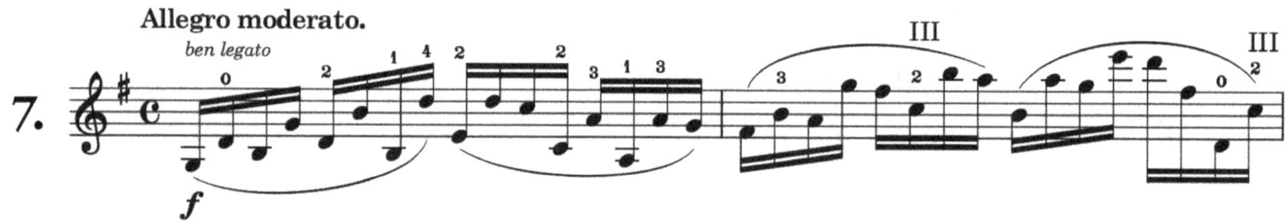

Prepare this caprice in double stops with precise and liquid calculation of its required shifting with the goal of developing both speed and accuracy.

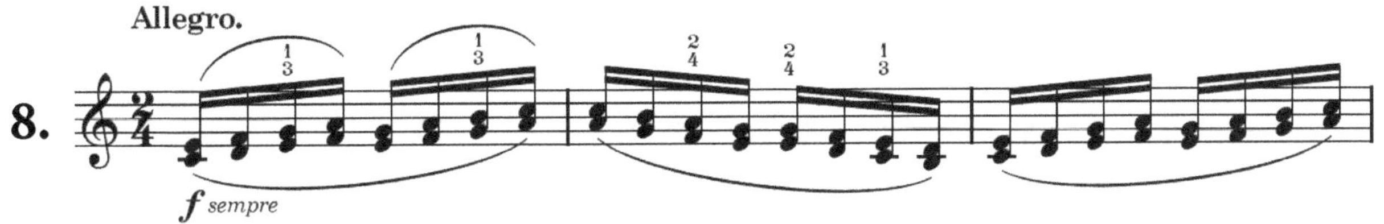

This caprice can easily be a "lifetime" etude to be played with both thirds and fingered octaves.

No. 13 combines the challenges of Dont Caprices No. 2 and No. 5 but with increased difficulty for both string crossings and alacrity.

The arpeggiated legato required for this caprice is challenging for both bow speed and bow changes. Accuracy in the left hand is achieved with crisp vertical finger motion juxtaposed with smooth arpeggiated shifting.

No. 18 is a good study for legato in double stop string crossings.

This caprice can be used in a variety of formats but eventually should be played very quickly and very accurately.

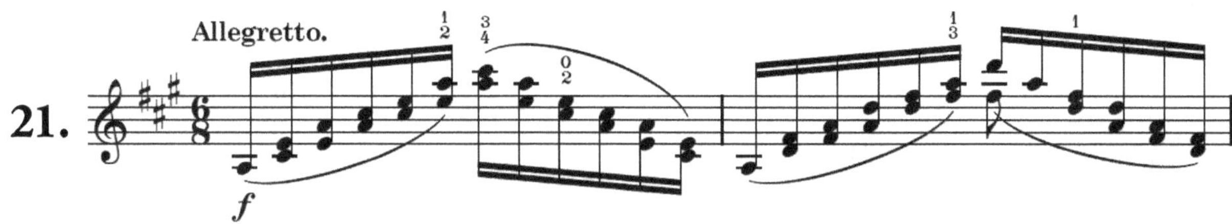

This caprice presents difficulties similar to those of caprice No. 18 but contains even more virtuoso challenges.

Part III:

Repertoire Progression

The following represents a general overview of a repertoire sequence that I have found to be useful. It is not intended to be a rigid system but it can provide a guideline when given with appropriate technical development. I very strongly feel that balanced preparation includes daily focus not only on a concerto or virtuoso piece but also on scales, etudes, and solo Bach.[7]

Concertos/Larger Works, grouped in stages of increasing technical development

Accolay	Violin Concerto No. 1 in A Minor
Bach	Violin Concerto No. 1 in A Minor
Handel	Violin Sonata in D Major, Op. 1 No. 4
Vivaldi	Sonata in D Major RV 10 (arr. Respighi)*
Ten Have	Allegro Brillante, Op. 19
Nardini	Concerto in E Minor*
Haydn	Violin Concerto No. 1 in C Major*
Haydn	Violin Concerto No. 2 in G Major
Mozart	Violin Concerto No. 2 in D Major, K. 211
Bach	Violin Concerto No. 2 in E Major
Viotti	Violin Concerto No. 22 in A Minor*
Viotti	Violin Concerto No. 23 in G Major*
Kabalevsky	Violin Concerto in C Major, Op. 48*
Kreisler	Praeludium and Allegro (in the style of Pugnani)
Kreisler	Sicilienne and Rigaudon (in the style of Francoeur)*

---

[7] See also "Appendix: Additional Commentary" on page 72

* Asterisk indicates editors' additions.

Notes to a Violinist

Bartók	Romanian Folk Dances
Beethoven	Romance No. 2 in F Major, Op. 50
Mozart	Adagio in E Major, K. 261
Mozart	Rondo in C Major, K. 373
Leclair	Sonata in D Major, Op. 9 No. 3*
Vitali	Chaconne
Tartini	Sonata in G Minor, "The Devil's Trill" (arr. Kreisler)*
Sinding	Suite in A Minor, Op. 10

❧

Bruch	Violin Concerto No. 1 in G Minor, Op. 26
Conus	Violin Concerto in E Minor
Khachaturian	Violin Concerto in D Minor*
Lalo	Symphonie Espagnole, Op. 21
Mendelssohn	Violin Concerto in E Minor, Op. 64
Saint-Saëns	Violin Concerto in No. 3 in B Minor, Op. 61
Wieniawski	Violin Concerto No. 2 in D Minor, Op. 22
Mozart	Violin Concerto No. 5 in A Major, K. 219

❧

Saint-Saëns	Introduction and Rondo Capriccioso, Op. 28
Chausson	Poème, Op. 25

Ravel	Tzigane
Saint-Saëns	Havanaise, Op. 83
Mozart	Violin Concerto No. 4 in D Major, K. 218

ঔ

Vieuxtemps	Violin Concerto No. 5 in A Minor, Op. 37
Paganini	Violin Concerto No. 1 in D Major, Op. 6
Wieniawski	Violin Concerto No. 1 in F# Minor, Op. 14

ঔ

Bruch	Scottish Fantasy, Op. 46
Tchaikovsky	Violin Concerto in D Major, Op. 35
Sibelius	Violin Concerto in D Minor, Op. 47
Dvořák	Violin Concerto in A Minor, Op. 53
Prokofiev	Violin Concerto No. 2 in G Minor, Op. 63
Glazunov	Violin Concerto in A Minor, Op. 82
Korngold	Violin Concerto in D Major, Op. 35
Brahms	Violin Concerto in D Major, Op. 77
Barber	Violin Concerto, Op. 14
Prokofiev	Violin Concerto No. 1 in D Major, Op. 19
Shostakovich	Violin Concerto No. 1 in A Minor, Op. 77

Bartók	Violin Concerto No. 2
Elgar	Violin Concerto in B Minor, Op. 61
Walton	Violin Concerto
Berg	Violin Concerto
Stravinsky	Violin Concerto in D Major
Beethoven	Violin Concerto in D Major, Op. 61

Virtuoso Pieces and Other Works[8]

Wieniawski

Polonaise No. 1 in D Major, Op. 4
Scherzo Tarantelle, Op. 16
Legende, Op. 17
Polonaise Brillante No. 2 in A Major, Op. 21

Ysaÿe

Six Sonatas for solo violin:
    Sonata No. 3 in D Minor, "Ballade"
    Sonata No. 6 in E Major
    etc.

---

[8] See also "Appendix: Additional Commentary" on page 72

Introduction and Tarantella, Op. 43
Zigeunerweisen, Op. 20
Carmen Fantasy, Op. 25

Paganini

Moto Perpetuo, Op. 11
La Campanella (arr. Kreisler)
Le Streghe (Witches' Dance), Op. 8
I Palpiti, Op. 13

Ernst

Variations on "The Last Rose of Summer"
Grand Caprice, Op. 26, on "Der Erlkönig" by Schubert

Waxman

Carmen Fantasie, based on themes from the opera by Bizet

Scriabin

Etude in Thirds (arr. Szigeti)

Sonatas

Mozart

Schubert

Fauré

Franck

Debussy

Ravel

Beethoven

Brahms

Bartók (Solo Sonata, Sonatas with piano)

Strauss

Prokofiev*

Schumann*

Solo Bach ....

This is an essential part of serious violin instruction and skill acquisition. The teacher is responsible for teaching Bach's intellectual and technical challenges, particularly emphasizing excellent tone production, while seeking the aesthetic and spiritual depths that make this music a rewarding and life-long journey.

An unaccompanied Bach sequence with each sonata/partita memorized and performed in its entirety:

- ℰ Partita No. 3 in E Major
- ℰ Sonata No. 1 in G Minor
- ℰ Partita No. 1 in B Minor
- ℰ Partita No. 2 in D Minor
- ℰ Sonata No. 2 in A Minor
- ℰ Sonata No. 3 in C Major

---

* Asterisk indicates editors' additions.

Closing Notes

Preparation for excellent performance requires both patience and persistence, *never* rigidity. Any worthwhile system sheds light on this process.

The teacher should encourage students to explore the art, literature, and culture of a work's era, using these resources to enrich a student's point of view in both preparation and performance.

Teachers must seek to develop and enable parameters for true artistic expression, resisting the imposition of the brittle and crippling orthodoxies which inhibit both musical and technical intent.

It is incumbent upon the teacher to recognize a student's current technical and artistic limitations and then be able to clearly articulate the steps needed for progress.

It is critically important that the teacher establish a unique, communicative relationship with each student. This makes possible the viability of achieving the technical and artistic command required for the demands of professional life.

Jan Mark Sloman

Appendix:
Additional Commentary

Jan Sloman made a concerted effort to provide regular performance opportunities for students, which included:

- Hosting studio recitals every month in his living room for friends and family, followed by a lively potluck reception in the kitchen

- Organizing guest master classes

- Organizing studio classes in conservatory and festival settings

- Directing his own summer chamber music program, The Institute For Strings (TIFS), which ran for nineteen seasons in Dallas.

"TIFS existed to prepare dedicated, hard-working students for the performing experience. Its programs gave young players an opportunity to work closely with experienced, dedicated coaches to develop the interactive skills and technical discipline that chamber music demands. The sessions offered chamber music study and performance, sonata class for selected participants, master classes and solo performance opportunities, large ensemble and musicians' chorus, and speakers on interdisciplinary activities related to performance." – description from Sloman's website, 2022

Sloman made it clear that building performance experience and endurance over time was an important part of students' development, which contributed greatly to their artistic growth and success.

In private lessons, Sloman's students generally worked on scales, etudes, and repertoire – which could include a major solo work with orchestra, a virtuoso piece, a sonata for violin and piano, and/or encore piece. Wieniawski and Sarasate virtuoso pieces might be studied around the same time as, or before, concerti such as Paganini's first concerto or Wieniawski's first concerto. Ysaÿe sonatas, other virtuosic pieces, and more complex sonatas would often be introduced around that time or afterward.

A short list of additional or encore pieces can be found below.

Bazzini	La ronde des lutins
Bloch	Nigun
Brahms	Sonatensatz (Scherzo from the F.A.E. Sonata)
Chopin	Nocturne in C# Minor (arr. Milstein)
Debussy	La fille aux cheveux de lin (arr. Hartmann) La plus que lente (arr. Roques)
Dvořák	Romance
Elgar	Salut d'amour
Engel	Sea-Shell (arr. Zimbalist)
Fiocco	Allegro in G Major
Nováček	Moto Perpetuo
Paradis	Sicilienne
Piazzolla	Nightclub 1960 from *Histoire du Tango*
Saint-Saëns	Danse macabre
Tchaikovsky	Mélodie from *Souvenir d'un lieu cher* Valse Sentimentale
Veracini	Largo
Wagner	Albumblatt, WWV 94

Transcriptions and arrangements by **Heifetz:**

Debussy	Beau soir
Dinicu	Hora Staccato
Gershwin	"Summertime" from *Porgy and Bess* "It Ain't Necessarily So" from *Porgy and Bess*
Prokofiev	March from *Love for Three Oranges*
Rimsky-Korsakov	Flight of the Bumblebee

Compositions, transcriptions, and arrangements by **Kreisler:**

Corelli	Sonata in D Minor, Op. 1, No. 12, "La Folia"
de Falla	Danse Espagnole from *La Vida Breve*
Gluck	Melodie from *Orfeo ed Euridice*
Kreisler	Cavatina La Chasse (in the style of Cartier) La Gitana Liebesleid Recitative and Scherzo Rondino on a Theme by Beethoven Tambourin Chinois Tempo di Minuetto (in the style of Pugnani) Variations on a Theme by Corelli (in the style of Tartini) Viennese Rhapsodic Fantasietta
Mozart	Rondo from "Haffner" Serenade, K.250
Wieniawski	Caprice No. 4 in A Minor

Notes to a Violinist

About the Author

Photo by Ed Hille

Jan Mark Sloman (1949–2022) was a highly regarded violinist and dedicated teacher whose multifaceted career reflected his passion for the violin, its ability to communicate powerfully, and his desire to develop true artistry in the students he guided. Based in Dallas, Texas, he held the position of Principal Associate Concertmaster of the Dallas Symphony Orchestra for thirty-eight years. He also performed as guest concertmaster with the Pittsburgh Symphony and with orchestras in Florence, Italy; Lugano and Geneva, Switzerland; and Melbourne, Australia. Over the course of his career he worked with world-renowned conductors, including Carlos Kleiber, Lorin Maazel, Zubin Mehta, and Riccardo Chailly.

Sloman mastered a wide range of repertoire as an orchestral soloist, ranging from Bach and Beethoven to Tippett and Shostakovich, and his recital and chamber music performances were highlighted by collaboration with artists such as Leonard Rose, Nobuko Imai, and Yo-Yo Ma. He was a University Scholar at Princeton University and later attended the Curtis Institute of Music, where he studied with the legendary twentieth-century pedagogue Ivan Galamian. His other teachers included Paul Makanowitzky, Sally Thomas, Jaime Laredo, and Joseph Silverstein.

Sloman's attention increasingly turned to teaching. He was appointed to the faculties of Southern Methodist University, the Cleveland Institute of Music, the Heifetz International Music Institute, and the Meadowmount School of Music, among others. He had a large private studio in Dallas and also embraced the digital world early on, adding teaching via Skype and mentoring students throughout the United States.

Strongly committed to educational opportunities for young musicians, Sloman founded and directed a nonprofit organization, The Institute for Strings, to provide students in the Dallas area the opportunity to immerse themselves in an intensive music program that included solo and chamber music performance opportunities, as well as concerts as part of a self-conducted string orchestra. This unique summer program allowed 40 elite string players each session the ability to work with experienced professional musicians to hone their technical and interactive music skills over the course of 19 seasons.

The success of Sloman's students at major conservatories and competitions brought him increasing national recognition as a teacher and mentor of the next generation of string players. His students have been finalists and received awards in both national and international competitions including: American String Teachers Association, Cooper, Davidson Institute, Fischoff, Kingsville, Music Teachers National Association, Sphinx, Stulberg, YoungArts, and Andrea Postacchini (Italy). Additionally, his students have won top prizes in the Queen Elisabeth, Sendai, Naumburg, Indianapolis, and Spohr Competitions. In 2004, he received the Pre-Collegiate Teaching Achievement award given by the Texas Music Teachers Association and in 2010 was named YoungArts Performing Arts Educator of the Year by the National Foundation for Advancement in the Arts.

Sloman in his home studio, 2003.

Master class in Córdoba, Spain, at the invitation of
Rubén Gallardo, 2006.

Point of view from a student "waiting in the wings"
at a studio recital in Dallas, 2011.